RESPECT

Category: Business & Economics

Description: You will learn how to earn the respect and trust of your customers by being an expert in your business. You will discover how to always be on the lookout for new ideas; new information and new products that will help your customers grow their business.

Copyright Bob Oros-2017
ISBN 978-1-105-22667-0

Written and published by Bob Oros
832 NW 142nd Street, Edmond, OK 73013
405-751-9191 Email Bob@BobOros.com
Web site www.BobOros.com

RESPECT 1

Respect: Earn respect by being an expert 6

One good reason 6

Product Knowledge is Important 13

Points of difference 17

I need business NOW 25

Guarantee your success 31

Sell loyalty not price 33

No 2 products are the same 38

The power of knowing 45

9. Respect: Earn respect by being an expert 55

My 4% improvement objective: 57

What the entire eBook series will do for you 59

Ben Franklin's system 60

Respect:
Earn respect by being an expert

One good reason

Give me one good reason why I should buy from you!

I get sales people calling me all the time. You all look alike - sound alike - make the same promises, what makes you any different?

You have to separate yourself from the competition. You have to be different.

You have to be better.

One of the best ways to separate yourself from the competition is to know everything there is to know about your products and services. If you know what you are talking about, the customer feels it and starts trusting what you say.

The goal is not necessarily to be able to give very technical characteristics. The goal is to know the product so much in depth that you are able to simplify the complicated characteristics into powerful advantages for the client to use the product. This means applying what you learn by turning your product knowledge into benefits and presenting these benefits to your customers.

Attend all the presentations, seminars, courses and talks by renowned speakers that are available. Don't consider these an expense, but an investment to better yourself.

You will always learn from these presentations, seminars, courses and talks. Accept all supplier invitations for sales, marketing or product information seminars.

When you have the opportunity to attend an industry convention or regional training function talk to people who are more successful than you are and learn everything you can from them.

After a while, from all the information you store in your mind from all these different sources, you develop your own style and your own recipes for success that work best for you. This is the unique strategy that will keep you one step ahead of your competition.

Learning and self-improvement implies one essential feeling: the desire to be better, the desire to improve.

Many sales people are often surprised to find themselves dropping behind their competitors, but when they examine themselves, they find that they have stopped growing because they have ceased their effort to keep up with new selling techniques, new products and new marketing strategies.

Some people are so busy trying to learn the "tricks of the trade", they never learn the trade. Your ability as a sales person is always on the move, either one way or the other. It is either getting better or getting worse. Everything you do not use is slipping away.

Some sales people complain about having to attend sales meetings or training seminars. Even if they knew everything offered by a training program, they still need the training. The essence of successful training is to build confidence by helping to improve the skills you already have.

Seminars and sales meetings are a great place to start, however, it is ultimately up to you to improve your skills. The person who continuously looks for new ideas and better methods of selling is the one who moves forward.

Commit to spending time every day learning more about your business. One hour a day spent studying your business will make you one of the top international experts in your field in 5 years.

One of the most successful sales people I know is a manufacturers rep for a seafood company. I first met him at a trade show where I asked him a question about a specific species of fish. He reached in his brief case and pulled out a 3 ring binder that was about 3 inches thick. This binder was filled with magazine articles, pictures, charts, newspaper clippings and notes that he had collected. He was continuously collecting information about his specialty. He was one of the most well informed sales people I have ever met, and is it any wonder he was so successful?

What are you doing to improve your knowledge and separate yourself from your competitor? I once looked at all the books on selling I had on my shelf and thought about how much useful information is in them yet going unused. I decided to do something bold. I took the books one by one and cut out all the things I wanted to learn and apply. I pasted the information on 3 x 5 cards and organized them by topic. I began reviewing them every day until I knew them and experienced what I had learned. Once you know something and then you do it with a conscious effort, you will really know it. Today, whenever I buy a book I buy two. One to keep and one to cut up.

It doesn't mater what system you use for increasing your knowledge bank, the important thing is that you learn and apply something new every day. A good place to start is by reading, absorbing and APPLYING the course you are now taking. As we previously discussed, APPLICATION is the key.

Product Knowledge is Important

A research firm sent questionnaires to 300 purchasing managers in various lines of business and the response was pretty interesting.   This group included 40 purchasing managers in the office equipment field, 25 distributor purchasing managers, 25 buyers of advertising and 200 purchasing managers of other types of businesses.   The questionnaire made the request that each person should set down the two or three qualifications he or she believed more essential than any others for a good sales person to possess. The following list shows the qualifications needed by sales people in order of their importance.

26% Product knowledge

17% Sincerity

16% Hard work

13% Honesty

07% Personality

07% Tact

04% Presentation ability

03% Ambition

03% Education

This is interesting information for you as a sales person. It helps put together a priority list for what to improve on. The first 3 are the most revealing, proving that you can't "wing it" with a professional purchasing manager – you have to know what you are talking about. You also have to be sincere, meaning that follow up and doing what you say will make a big difference on their decision to buy from you. This is something that cannot be avoided even if you think it is not necessary. And hard work (making prospecting calls and follow up calls) is what it takes to get and keep the business.

These numbers also put in place the idea that a "back slapping overly friendly personality" is not enough to get and keep the business. This also points out that product knowledge is more important than a flashy presentation with a lot of hype and bells and whistles. These numbers make it a priority to pay attention and be excited about attending your next product training or sales meeting.

Why is product knowledge so important? Let's make some calls on a few restaurants:

You call on a BBQ restaurant. You need to know why a pork butt is called a "Boston" butt. What is the difference between a back rib, a spare rib and St Louis rib.

You call on steak house. You need to know the difference between a yield grade 2 and a yield grade 3 and how it effects their food cost. You need to know all the benefits of a branded program.

You call on a pizza shop. You need to know the cost difference between the different slice counts on pepperoni, the benefits of precooked toppings vs. cooking their own.

You call on a nursing home. You need to know why a 22/26 slice count bacon will save them over $500 a year if they are using an 18/22 slice count.

You go to a seafood restaurant. You need to know what causes "mushy" fillets, how much breading is on the shrimp you are selling and what causes "belly burn."

You call on a deli. You need to know the difference between hard salami and Genoa salami, what "cotto" salami is and how much water is in the ham you are selling.

You call on a Mexican restaurant. You need to know what the cheese market is doing and how you can deliver their corn chips without getting broken.

The point is this. You have to know, really know, what you are talking about. You have to learn something every day that will make your career in sales the most interesting thing you can possibly do.

Points of difference

It's true! You can't sell anybody anything, you can't change people's minds, you can't persuade them to do something against their will and you can't get people to buy based on price alone.

We have to be crystal clear about what our job really is. We think that we have to apply pressure, use special psychological techniques and force people to buy from us.

Regardless of whether you are a supervisor, a sales person, a waitress, a service provider or a marketing manager your job is the same: Your job is to help people make good decisions - and the more informed you are about your products and services, the more valuable you are to your customer.

You can make your life a whole lot easier starting right now by stop thinking that you have to be clever and use some secret selling technique to get people to buy from you. All you have to do is answer this question; why should I buy from you? When someone asks that question of you what they are really asking is "I need help making a good decision!"

You might sell the exact same thing as everyone else, but you point out the differences of why your product or service is unique to their business. Sure everyone else is selling the same thing; however, what makes yours different is you have asked your clients about what they want from the product. You have listened and taken notes and figured out what your customer is trying to accomplish. You then give the customer the solution to their problem. The best part is, it has not cost you anything because you are not charging extra, just helping the customer make a good decision. You are adding value.

The "point of difference" of your product is the extra service you offer. This extra, in a sense, is your consulting service. And as a customer, when I can get free consulting service with a product or service the decision of who to buy from is easy. Even if it is a meal in a restaurant.

The secret of persuading people is that there is no secret. Just call on enough people and show them why doing business with you is the best decision they can possibly make! And if everything is equal, the deciding factor will be the fact that YOU go with the deal.

How am I supposed to learn everything about the products I sell when there is so much confusing information that I have to muddle through?

The answer - points of difference.

To increase your product knowledge, compare points of difference in the products. Each point of difference can be viewed as positive or negative depending on what your customer is looking for. Each point will change the price and the value of the product.

Considering the number of line items it takes to maintain a competitive inventory, gaining sufficient product knowledge is a long, slow process. With new products and programs being introduced continuously and old ones being changed or discontinued, it becomes a real challenge to stay on top of the necessary information.

The secret of gaining product knowledge is to compare points of difference. What is the difference between the new and the old? What is the difference between your product and a competitor's product? Each point of difference will change the price and the value of the product.

As a professional sales person you must be able to sell value added products. What kind of definition would you come up with when you are asked the meaning of "Value Added Selling"?

The best answer is to know the points of difference and sell your differences as a benefit.

A sales person who can answer objections with good solid facts and product information will out perform the person who "wings it" every time.

To gain the respect of your customers and earn their business, product knowledge should be a daily activity.

To increase product knowledge continually ask questions that help customers make the right choices. Read the trade journals and clip articles that contain helpful information for your customers.

All product knowledge has to be translated into customer benefits if it is to be of value to the customer. When selling, it does little good to focus on the features of the products or services offered. It makes little difference how long your company has been in business, how large your facility is, or how many employees you have unless it can be used to solve your customers problems.

Here is how you might use this to raise the bar on your own services. Take out any one of your software boxes, or stop in the computer store and browse through the software department. Notice how they are always comparing the old version with the new upgraded version. What would an upgraded version of YOU look like? What points of difference would there be between the old you and the you that you will become with just a slight nudge?

Here are a few examples:

The old version of you compared to the new version of you

OLD - Not excited about what I do
NEW - Really excited about my profession

OLD - Take care of my customers
NEW - Give extraordinary customer service

OLD - Only put in enough effort to get buy
NEW - Always go the extra mile for every customer

OLD - Customers know I appreciate them
NEW - Go out of my way to say thanks and show appreciation for my customers

When selling yourself and your services you must be able to convince your prospective customer that you are the right choice, you must know your strengths and be sure you transmit them so the message is received. Your customers can buy products from anyone. In an industry where everyone is selling the same products the most important point of difference is you. YOU are the customer's link to the universe. YOU are the one thing that really makes a difference. This puts a responsibility on you to be recourse - a problem solver. A typical sales person focuses on price while a true consultant finds out from the customer what he or she wants and helps them get it. That's how you earn their respect.

I need business NOW

Trying to skip the most important ingredient in opening a new account is a huge mistake many new sales people make.

Also, when you are put under pressure to make a sale, this step is not considered important - so it is skipped and the sale is lost. Nearly 100% of the time. The way things are out there today this essential ingredient is so important you wouldn't last a month as a new sales person unless you realize how important it is. You are under the gun for more sales. You call on a prospect, dump your sales pitch in their lap and wonder why they don't jump on board with you. You even cut the price so low you are not making any money. They still don't bite. And you wonder how people can be so set in their ways that they won't buy from you. You start looking for someone to blame. You think that your company doesn't offer the right products, or the service is not good enough. Your prices are too high! Well, all you have to do to see the problem is look in the mirror. And then ask yourself "why should anyone buy from me?" "I'm honest" you might say. "I work for a good company" you might be thinking. "I know my products inside and out" you might be saying, trying to justify your lack of sales. Well, all those things are important, but they don't matter all that much. Just about everyone in sales has the same things going for them. Let's look at it from the prospect's point of view. "I don't care how low your prices are. I don't care how many benefits you have. I don't care if you have the most perfect offer in the universe. I don't know you - so I don't trust you. Period!" So, Job 1 is to establish trust.

You MUST establish trust if you want to make the sale. And today people don't trust anybody unless they have earned it and neither should you. Here is the one way guaranteed to build trust. And if you are a buyer, don't buy unless you established trust with the person doing the selling. In today's economy everybody is under the gun. They feel the pressure. The heat is on and some people don't know how to deal with it.

The only way to build trust today is consistent exposure. Consistent exposure means that you make the first call and pick up some information. It means on the second call you pick up a little more information. It means on the third call you bring them an idea that will help their business. On the forth call you bring them a sample. On the fifth call you bring them some helpful news, etc. I know what you are thinking. I need business NOW.

I just lost one of my biggest accounts. My income is going to take a huge cut. Well, you should have thought of that 21 weeks ago. That is how many exposures it takes today before someone will really trust you enough to give you their business. Let me say that again. TWENTY-ONE exposures! Are you so confident that you don't need to call on any new business? Are you so sure about your current customers that you know they will never leave you, never go out of business, never switch ownership, or a dozen other reasons that can cause you to lose a customer? Are you thinking that because your title is Territory Manager, Marketing Associate, District Sales Manager, Account Manager, Area Manager, General Manager, etc. that your job description is not SELLING? Are you embarrassed to be called a sales person? If you are, you are missing the whole point of being in business. Those titles are not designed to exclude you from selling; they are there so make the customer view you as something other than someone who is simply trying to sell them something.

But from your point of view, you need to say to yourself "I am a sales person and damn proud of it!" What does this mean in sales activities? It means you better add 10 more prospects to your list and start a "consistent exposure" program with each of them. It means you better not take your current customers for granted. It means you had better be a little more demanding of yourself. It means that if you are not putting in a 50 to 60 hour week you are not doing the job that needs to be done. You are not pulling your share of the effort it is going to take to pull your company out of the negative situation it is in. It means you are a drag on the system. Trust. You need to be establishing it at a deeper level than ever. It is not who has the cheapest price! It's who do I trust the most with my business?

There are a lot of scammers out there.

Every night on the news you hear about another way someone was taken advantage of, lost their money, lost their house, lost their business, etc. More and more reasons not to trust anyone. And in walks you! You want me to dump my current vendor and you want me to buy from you! How do I know you are who you say you are? How do I know you have my interest at heart? How do I know you will deliver what you say you will? Those things have to be earned. After I see you consistently 21 times and you have followed up on some of the things I have asked you about. After you bring me references and testimonials from people I know - and I check you out, then we can talk. Then we will have established a relationship based on mutual trust. Then we can do some business. Try to high pressure me into giving you an order before you have earned it and you might as well never come back. You might as well go work for the government. Because trying to sell in today's business climate without first earning trust is like having the most powerful computer in the world and not knowing that you have to plug it in to make it work! And by the way. The 21 exposures comes from the National Advertising

Association. That's how many exposures it takes before someone will trust you enough to buy!

Guarantee your success

Do you know that it is IMPOSSIBLE to fail? It is impossible to persistently apply and reapply the principles of selling and fail. It can't be done!

Application of selling principles is the key. Many sales people talk a good game. They can tell you about the big sale they almost made, the hot new account they are working on, or the big sales goal they have. They can talk a good game with their customers as well.

"Sure, I will get back to you on that."

"Trust me, this is the product and program for you."

You know the type. The person who continuously looks for new ideas and better methods of selling is the one who moves forward. The person who learns something new, applies it and reapplies it over and over until it becomes a skill. The person who DOES what he or she says they are going to do is the one who makes it in the long run.

Customers are not sold by empty promises made by sales people who are insincere - they are sold by a sales person who WEARS WELL. The person who looks for ways to show their customers how to make more money, how to sell more, how better manage their business, is the person who is not full of hot air and promises.

To be the type of person who wears well all you have to do is simply... DO WHAT YOU SAY YOU WILL DO. Apply what you learn and then reapply it again and again until it is automatic.

The toughest door to open is the one that gets us out of the house early and the toughest sale is the one we have to make to ourselves. We have to convince ourselves to do what we learn until we own the skill, to apply what may seem difficult at first.

There is no magic rabbit that you pull out of the hat and say "here is the secret of selling." There is no silver bullet that will win the sale every time. However, it is impossible to persistently apply and reapply the principles of selling and fail.

Sell loyalty not price

When you train your customers to buy based on price, they become loyal to the price, and not loyal to you.

For example, if a new giant retailer came into the marketplace today and their whole sales pitch was "We promise to be THE lowest-priced store in town -- we will even beat WAL-MART hands-down, on every single item in stock."

What do you think would happen? Do you think everyone would stay put and stay faithful to Wal-Mart? I doubt it. Sure you'd have a few die-hards, but for the most part, Wal-Mart's customers would RUN as fast as they can to this new store.

Building loyalty to YOU is far more important, and makes pricing FAR less important, however, if you want that kind of loyalty, you have to earn it!

Here is a step-by-step plan for earning loyalty...

First of all you have to really know your products. You have to know what makes them tick. You have to know them inside and out. You have to know WHY they are priced where they are. You have to know the difference between the quality of the cheap product compared to the more expensive product. In other words, you have to do your homework. You have to look forward to your sales meetings and training programs excited that you will pick up a small piece of information that you did not previously know. You have to learn all the points of difference in your products, your competitors product as well as the different quality levels of your own product.

Now, you are in front of a customer and he or she says "I can buy that from your competitor a lot cheaper!" If you have done your homework you will know how to respond. If you have the product "points of difference" clearly defined in your mind as well as the "points of difference" between your company and your competitor's company, a customer response like this is welcomed. It is not a dead end.

Let's go back to Wal-Mart for an example.

I walk a lot. Depending on the weather, one or two miles a day. I needed a new pair of walking shoes, so I wandered into the Wal-Mart shoe department while my wife did some shopping. There they were! A great looking pair of walking shoes for only $12! Think of it? Twelve bucks! I tried them on and they fit perfectly. I bought some inserts for a little more support and walked out of the store with a new pair of shoes for less than $20.

Forty-five days later they were in the trash and I had a case of plantar fasciitis! I didn't know what it was either until my right foot started hurting so bad I could hardly stand on it. It was caused by the lack of support from the shoes.

Do you think I will ever buy a pair of walking shoes at Wal-Mart again, even if they were five dollars? Not a chance!

I went to a shoe store and talked with a sales person who really knew his products. He explained what plantar fasciitis was and how it happens after about six week of walking in cheap shoes. I paid five times more for a good pair of shoes and will never buy a cheap pair again.

Let's look at how you present your products and services. Do you always lead with price? Do you say, "we have the cheapest products in town?" Do you always back down when a customer says your prices are too high?

So, getting back to building loyalty to YOU and not to PRICE. Here's how you do it. Every time you talk with a customer your job is to educate them. Your job is a teacher. If you take the educational route you will be training and preparing your customers for higher prices and higher values. Every time a customer visits your store or restaurant you and your staff should have a product teaching segment. "Here is a high quality item. Let me show you why you get so much value when you purchase it."

Wal-Mart trains you to buy on price. In reality they roll back one while they roll up another. Or they sell merchandise that is so low in quality it doesn't last. That may work for a giant retailer with unlimited resources, but it's a slow death for a small business, restaurant or retail store.

There will always be price shoppers. It's part of the way things work. But don't let them give you the idea that doing business today is only about price. It's your job to teach and train your customers with good solid facts, figures and product knowledge. Your job is NOT about using sales gimmicks or fancy marketing techniques or bait and switch tactics that everyone is using these days.

Your job it to increase sales by teaching, by consulting, by learning your product line, by selling the value, by selling return-on-investment, not simply quoting price.

Regardless of whether you are selling shoes or lobster tail and prime rib, sell the value and build loyalty to you, not to the price.

No 2 products are the same

We have two boxes of commodity product; let's use chicken breasts as an example. (This could be any product or service). Both processed or manufactured by the same company. You are the distributor sales person selling one case. Your competitor is the distributor sales person selling the other case. Your price is higher.

What do you do? Lower your price to meet your competitor and take a hit on your profit? Call your buyer and tell him or her they are paying too much? Call the manufacturer and complain that your competitor is getting better pricing?

No. Here is what you have to do if you want to continue to have credibility with the customer.

You have to become a detective and find out all the facts. You have to do some homework. Once you do your homework you will have the answer and will know what to do the next time it happens.

Here are the questions you have to ask:

What else was shipped with the product? For example did they buy some cleaning chemicals with a high gross profit allowing them to lower the price on the chicken breast?

Did they have some temporary marketing money they used to apply to the product to lower the price?

Are they using the product as a "loss leader" to take the business away by selling on price?

Did you check the label to be SURE they are the same? If there are two establishment numbers they were processed at two different processing plants. This could affect the price.

Are you SURE one is not a random size and the other is an exact size?

Are you SURE nothing has been added such as marinade or water?

Are you SURE one has not been organically raised while the other was not?

Have you checked the processing date to see if one is older than the other?

Is this the first time your competitor has offered this product at this price?

So far you find that everything checks out. What's next?

Have all the "hidden" costs been added in.

Are you the customer's regular vendor and selling them most of their items? If so and your competitor is trying to cherry pick your business, creating another vendor for the customer to deal with, the cost just went up. Why? The average cost of processing a vendor invoice is approximately $80.00. That cost has to be added to the price.

Is the customer paying C.O.D. for the competitor's product and you are giving them 14 or 21 days?

Are you printing their menus, providing manufacturer rebates and offering marketing services while your competitor is not?

Are you providing two deliveries per week and your competitor is providing one per week?

Are you showing up in person while your competitor is simply calling on the phone or sending a fax/email with pricing?

Did they pick the product up at Sam's Club and didn't add in the cost of going to pick it up?

If they picked it up at Sam's Club did they buy a whole bunch of stuff they didn't plan on buying when they walked through the store? Did you add those to the price?

Do you guarantee the quality to be perfect and your competitor is selling with no return policy?

If the order is out of stock on the delivery day will your competitor call, let the customer know and find a substitute product at another account to make sure they are covered. And if that does happen will you call the customer in advance to let them know while your competitor simply ignores the problem?

Does your customer have 24/7 access to you via your cell phone and your competitor disappears every Friday at noon and can't be found until Monday morning?

Do you offer your services as a professional consultant by showing your customer how to have over 25 menu items from that single chicken breast and your competitor just drops the box and says "see ya later?"

Do you help your customer set their prices so they will make more money selling the product, far out weighing the few dollars they are going to save buying the cheaper competitor's price?

Do you go beyond the product and offer them help on how to market their entire company?

Do you have a team of specialists who you can call on to come in to your customer and offer a variety of services from wait staff training to lowering their electric bills?

Have you let the customer know, not by what you say but by what you have done, that you go with every box and YOU make a real difference by the VALUE YOU BRING TO THE TABLE? Again, not by what you say, but by what you have DONE!

Do these two boxes still look the same?

You will never earn the respect of your customer if you don't know how to present the "points of difference" between you and your competitor. If you don't know how to sell the VALUE that goes with everything you sell in an honest and professional way. If you don't know how to keep the interest of your customer as your highest priority. If you don't know how to really create value and be proud of your price because you know it is worth every penny. If you think that a cheap price and an inferior product is the only way to get a sale.

The power of knowing

IS IT POSSIBLE TO DESCRIBE A PLACE YOU HAVE NEVER BEEN?

I was driving down highway 75 in Florida and pulled off at a Long John Silver seafood restaurant for lunch. As I was entering the front door a 'pan handler' was sitting on the curb asking everyone for their spare change. As I was eating lunch I could see him through the window and I thought how distracting it was to the customers. I wondered why the manager didn't ask him to leave. He had a can in front of him and one out of every five people dropped some change in it. I got to thinking that one out of every five is a pretty good closing ratio. One more confirmation of the 2 out of every 10 law.

After I finished eating I walked out the door and was thinking about how I was going to avoid him. I was dressed extremely casual as my whole day consisted of simply driving from point A to point B. I have special cloths for these occasions as I don't want to travel with a whole lot of luggage. So I have some old jeans and a special sweat shirt that my wife keeps telling me to throw away. As we made eye contact I made a spur-of-the-moment decision. I sat on the curb next to him. For the next 30 minutes I learned five lessons that will stay with me for a long time. Because of those 30 minutes I am not only a better sales person and a better speaker, I am a better person.

The first lesson I learned was how it feels when someone thinks you are a bum asking for a handout. It was a strange feeling. I wanted to tell these folks who were walking by that I was not with this guy. I was just talking with him. I am not a beggar. I work for a living. Some of them looked disgusted. It was as if they were silently telling us to get a job. One irate man said that he would give us a couple of bucks but he rudely accused us of being a couple of drunks and the money would just be wasted. Some people avoided eye contact with us all together. I guess they felt that if they locked eyes with either of us they would feel an obligation to put some money in the can. After the first five minutes the concern about what people thought left me. They don't know who I am. They will never see me again. I wondered what they would think when they see me walk over to my rental car and put the top down on my convertible!

It is hard to put into words the transformation I went through after I told myself; "so what if they think I'm a bum – that's their problem, not mine!" I may have made this adjustment a lot quicker than the average person because I had sales experience I could draw on. One of the most difficult obstacles a beginning sales person has to overcome is the concern he or she has about what people will think of them. If you are not making the calls because you are worried about what someone will think about you, here is some important insight. They are not thinking about you. They are thinking about themselves. Do you think the people who walked by me went in the restaurant and thought about me during their entire meal? The amount of time they spent thinking about me could be measured in fractions of a second. Yet, most of the reason many sales people do not reach their full selling potential is because they are dominated by this concern about what people will think.

The second lesson was that one out of every five people dropped some change in the can. I thought that was really interesting. He didn't even have to say anything, the can was the presentation! The can did the job for him. He completely set the stage for the sale. He was appropriately dressed to look like a street person. There was no question about it. His old sneakers, his faded shirt which was covered by his sleeveless sweater, his baseball hat, his unshaven face, all creating the perfect appearance of what the ideal homeless person looked like in the eyes of his "customer." And because of this carefully designed "theater" he set up, one out of five were convinced that the right thing to do was to help him (us) out. This was an interesting observation. In my experience if you look like a sales person, the sale is harder to make. If you look like someone who is there to help solve a problem, you have successfully set the stage for a sale, and it comes much easier. Try changing your image from a stereotype sales person to a problem solver and see how much more receptive your customers will be. When you go to the gatekeeper and ask to see the manager don't introduce yourself as a sales person. Instead introduce yourself as a problem solver. When you are asked what is this about, answer by telling them you don't know until you ask them 3 simple questions and it takes less that three minutes.

The third lesson was that he said thanks to everyone. Not just the words thank you, but a sincere - I really appreciate it - thank you. He made them feel good about putting money in his can. People like to help other people, or at least one out of five do, as my research proved. Did you ever wonder what people think about after they buy something from you? They don't really expect any gratitude on the surface. But deep down inside they're screaming to be appreciated. It is very rare for us to get the red carpet treatment from anyone. I recently visited a store and was shocked by the excellent service. Someone met us at the door, escorted us through the isles, answered our questions, gave us snacks to eat while we were shopping, and when we checked-out, you won't believe what happened! They wrote down our name, address and birthday. Two days later we got a thank you card in the mail and a birthday card followed a few days before the big day. Now, the thing that made this so special was "we" were my dog and I. It was a pet store and that's how they treated my DOG! Do you really appreciate your customers? I mean REALLY?

The forth lesson. Here is his story. His name is Ralph and he lived in South Carolina. He lost his job and on the very same day his wife left him. She cleaned out their apartment, their bank accounts and maxed all the credit cards by taking cash advances. He was left with the cloths he had in the apartment closet and about $20 in his pocket. He had no family so he packed a small suit case and went to the local truck stop where he hitched a ride to Florida. He had been there a month when I ran into him. I asked him all the questions you would ask. Have you looked for a job? "I can't even get a job as a day laborer without a Florida address. I have no transportation, no place to live, no friends, no credit and no money. All I can do is find some place to set up for the day and see if enough folks will help me so I can buy a meal." He spends every night trying to find a place to unroll his sleeping bag. The lesson that Ralph taught me was this: I have absolutely nothing to complain about. Nothing! I stood up to leave, opened my wallet and gave

Ralph fifty dollars. That was by far the best sales, marketing and motivation training I have ever received in my entire life.

The fifth lesson. Even though I talked with Ralph for 30 minutes, and for a moment knew the feeling of what it was like to be perceived as a street person, I couldn't begin to describe what it must be like to live on the street.

Why?

Because it is impossible to describe a place you have never been. Before someone assumes the role of teacher or trainer they have to know – really know – what they are talking about. They cannot spend 30 minutes next to a client or customer on a curb asking questions and think they know what it is like to have the problems they are dealing with.

You see, a consultant really has to KNOW. Let me give you an example of KNOWING.

The manager of a school cafeteria has to KNOW this. Let's say the holidays are approaching and the manager is going to cook turkeys for the school kids. The turkeys are stuffed the night before and put in the refrigerator over night. The result: putting warm stuffing in a cold turkey overnight will cause botulism spores to grow which will create a toxin that cannot be killed by cooking. If there are onions in the stuffing they will accelerate the growth of the spores. The turkeys are cooked the next day and the school kids get sick. If they are not rushed to the hospital the toxin will cause the children to die with botulism poisoning.

Anything less than this type of KNOWING is the same as trying to tell someone how it feels to live on the street based on a chance conversation with a person who IS living on the street.

I don't know what if feels like to live on the street, but I DO KNOW what the pain of defeat and sting of rejection feels like! I DO know what it feels like to be turned down over and over again yet picking yourself up and keep on going, I DO know what it's like to live out of a suit case for weeks at a time traveling from airport to airport, dealing with over crowded airplanes, navigating rental cars in strange cities, calling on pressured and short tempered buyers and purchasing agents, up late wining and dining, only to leave the next morning on the 6:00 o'clock flight to do it all over again! These are the things I can say I REALLY KNOW!

This is what it means for me to EARN YOUR RESPECT BY BEING AN EXPERT!

9. Respect: Earn respect by being an expert

I have earned the respect and trust of my customers by being an expert in my business. I am always on the lookout for new ideas; new information and new products that will help my customers grow their business. I read the trade journals, I study new products, I watch my competition and I am a valuable source of news and information for my customers. I can be trusted with confidential information my customers share with me and I never engage in gossip or criticism about other people or other companies. I never put down my competition or the competition of my customers. Because of this integrity my customer has complete confidence in me and respect for the way I conduct my business.

My 4% improvement objective:

What the entire eBook series will do for you

Buying all 13 books is like buying a library of 13 powerful coaching sessions that will increase every skill necessary for generating business. Once you experience the seemingly effortless improvement you will understand why there is a picture of Ben Franklin on every 100 dollar bill.

You will learn how to improve relationships, improve management skills, be more productive, generate more customers, negotiate better contracts, open new accounts, earn more profits and create more sales! Results most people only dream about! If you are a sales professional or an entrepreneur this is the perfect program to boost your sales and increase your profits.

Ben Franklin's system

In our fast paced business and personal life today it has become increasingly difficult to set aside time for self development and improving your skills. With every spare minute taken up by reading blogs, logging on to Facebook, following people on Twitter, responding to text messages and emails and constantly talking on your cell phone, there seems to be little, if any, time left for learning new skills. Even the quiet time behind the wheel of your car is no longer available with satellite radio and cell phone coverage in every corner of the country.

Even though this seems like a new problem, distractions have been around forever. Two hundred years ago a man by the name of Ben Franklin had the same problem. He concluded that it was not a matter of distractions as much as a matter of focus. He set out to solve the problem and created the most effective system for self improvement ever invented.

Ben Franklin gives credit for all his success and accomplishments to the implementation of this system for the success he sought after. Despite being born into a poor family and only receiving two years of formal schooling, Ben Franklin became a successful printer, scientist, musician, author and one of the founding fathers of the United States. Ben Franklin is considered to have been one of the most persuasive and successful people in the history of the United States. He was a very skilled sales person, marketer, negotiator and copywriter. Skills that every business owner, professional person, manager and marketer should have.

In the year 1723, Ben Franklin, at the age of seventeen, arrived in Philadelphia without a penny to his name. At age 42, he retired, wealthy, the first self made millionaire in the country. Few people, before or since have ever been as successful as Benjamin Franklin. He gave credit for his many inventions and business successes to his system for self improvement he created when he was 20 years old.

The key to Franklin's success was his drive to constantly improve himself and accomplish his ambitions. In order to accomplish his goal, Franklin developed and committed himself to a personal improvement program that consisted of mastering 13 principles.

When he was seventy-nine years old, Benjamin Franklin wrote more about this idea than anything else that ever happened to him in his entire life. He felt that he owed all his success and happiness to this one thing. Franklin wrote: "I hope, therefore, that some of my descendants may follow the example and reap the benefit."

Since success is developed by performing small and seemingly insignificant acts, you can use this method by reading and putting into practice the 13 skills that will guarantee your success in sales with scientific certainty.

This program takes advantage of Franklin's system and applies it to improving your skills as a sales professional. This program will show you how to dominate your market by first dominating yourself. By focusing on the 13 skills that make up a highly effective and successful sales professional. As these skills are improved your results and sales increases will also show a dramatic improvement.

The goal of going through the program the first time is to increase each skill by only four percent. With the accomplishment of this small improvement in each skill or attitude your overall improvement will be 52%. Those are results most people only dream about. However, you can accomplish this by investing as little as 45 minutes once a week reading one book and then focusing on improving the single skill during the rest of the week. The second week by reading the second book and focusing on that single skill during the week and so on until all 13 weeks are completed.

You can write the single word on the back of your business card and tape it to your dash board as a reminder. You can put this one word on your smart phone as a reminder as well as on your email signature, your Facebook page or you can even have something worthwhile to tweet about. One word, one week, one skill, one "I am" statement, 4% improvement objective and your subconscious mind will receive the message through all the clutter and act on it.

After the first time through the process you can do as Ben Franklin suggests and go through the program a second, third and fourth time. Get your whole sales team on the same page at the same time and you will experience a whirlwind of new excitement and new business. Or get a like minded colleague and join forces with accountability and focus.

Achieve a 52% improvement

Using Franklin's scientific program for learning your objective is to improve 4% in each area over 13 weeks.

1. Attitude Define what you want and go after it.
2. Respect Earn respect-no more comfort zone.
3. Service Help customers build their business.
4. Urgency Be enthusiastic get things done now.
5. Confidence Remove restrictions and limitations.
6. Persistence Keep going and never give up.
7. Planning Get big results by setting big goals.
8. Questions Ask questions that make the sale.
9. Attention Get attention with irresistible offers.
10. Presenting Give reasons why they should buy.
11. Objections Remove every roadblock to the sale.
12. Closing Ask for the order and get paid.
13. Follow up Remove all hope for competitors.

About the author Bob Oros (BobOros.com),

Bob Oros has been a full time speaker and author since 1992 with over 2,000 speaking engagements in all 50 states and several international locations as well as the author of 21 books on sales. Prior to starting his speaking career, Bob served six years in the US Navy as a Communications Specialist and then worked his way from a street sales person to the position of National Sales Manager for a Fortune 200 company.

CSP Award: Bob was awarded the designation of Certified Speaking Professional (CSP) by the National Speakers Association and the International Federation for Professional Speakers. Fewer than 10% of all speakers worldwide qualify for this award.

PWA Member: Bob is a member of the Professional Writers Alliance.

www.ingramcontent.com/pod-product-compliance
Lightning Source LLC
Chambersburg PA
CBHW070432180526
45158CB00017B/981